What Color Is God's Love? is dedicated to Xavier, Arriana, and Xarian Dixon.
I thank God for Dr. Alan Dixon, Sr., Cendy Trujillo, "Mama Jana" Engelmann,
Tim Beals, Karen Neumair, and Bunmi Ishola, who believe in me,
encourage me, and pray for me as I write to worship God.
To God be the glory, the honor, and the praise!
—XD

To Mama and Papa, for believing in me.
—DV

WHAT COLOR IS GOD'S LOVE?

written by
XOCHITL DIXON

WATERBROOK

illustrated by
DARSHIKA VARMA

We know and rely on the love God has for us.
God is love. Whoever lives in love lives in God,
and God in them.

—1 JOHN 4:16

All the colors displayed in this world that God made—
every glorious, fabulous, beautiful shade—
show how good God *is* and will *always* be.

But what is the color of love? Come and see!

Is love orange like a pumpkin God grows from a seed
or like monarch butterflies that munch on milkweed?

ORANGE makes me feel grateful for the things God creates,
from the people we love to the food on our plates.

Is love yellow like the sunflowers God made to stand tall
or like honeysuckle vines that crawl up a wall?

YELLOW brings me joy, like friends working together
while God grows our garden in bright sunny weather.

Is love blue like the ocean or crystal-clear skies
or like blueberries picked for sweet homemade pies?

BLUE makes me feel calm, like a great day to set sail,
like a cool, peaceful breeze that says, "God will not fail."

Is love green like the clovers that tickle bare toes
or like frogs by a creek where a giant fern grows?

GREEN gives me confidence, so I'm ready to try.
With God, I can climb mountains, no matter how high.

Is love pink like flamingos or a puppy's wet tongue
or like cherry blossom trees that prove spring has sprung?

PINK sparks my imagination. I dare to dream bolder.
I'll serve God with my gifts now and when I'm older.

Is love black like the night sky where God hung the moon,
or like shiny-winged blackbirds that sing a sweet tune?

BLACK makes me courageous, so I stand up to fear.
I'm brave. I don't quit, because God's always near.

Is love white like the dandelion puffs that I blow
or like fluffy clouds floating across the sky slow?
WHITE helps me keep going when the day feels too rough.
No matter what happens, God is always enough.

Is love gray like a squirrel snoozing high in a tree
or like a chinchilla with fur soft as can be?

GRAY makes me feel hopeful because God controls
when lightning bolts strike and when loud thunder rolls.

Is love brown like the cross on the roof of God's house
or like the hay bed of a scurrying field mouse?

BROWN fills me with compassion, as God loves us all
and helps us love others through acts big and small.

Is love red like a rose God designed with great care
or like the thin, spiny skin of a prickly pear?

RED helps me remember I'm forgiven and free.
God, help me forgive others like You forgive me.

Is love purple like the robes choirs wear as they sing
of a big empty tomb and a great risen King?

PURPLE reminds me of all God gave through the Cross.
He helps me live like I know that Jesus is boss!

God uses all of His glorious colors to show
we can stay close to Him and continue to grow.

In all we say, do, and think, God helps us to see
His colors of love shining through you and through me.

Be devoted to one another in love.
Honor one another above yourselves.
—ROMANS 12:10

A NOTE FROM THE AUTHOR

Thank you for joining me as we celebrate the way God uses color to show His creativity and love for diversity in every aspect of His glorious creation. The following activity and questions are meant to encourage you to explore the spectacular colors in God's wonderful world.

ACTIVITY

Walk around your community with a trusted adult and find items that match the different colors described in *What Color Is God's Love?* Take photos of these items, draw them, make a list of them, or collect them. You can also invite one or more friends to help you create a collage or poster that shows your favorite discoveries in God's colorful world. You can even enjoy a colorful snack during your adventure!

QUESTIONS

What are your favorite colors?

How do these colors make you feel?

How can these colors remind you of God's love for you?

How can these colors remind you to love others?

Text copyright © 2024 by Xochitl Dixon
Cover art and interior illustrations copyright © 2024 by Darshika Varma

Published in the United States by WaterBrook, an imprint of Random House, a division of Penguin Random House LLC.

WaterBrook and its colophon are registered trademarks of Penguin Random House LLC.

ISBN 978-0-593-57901-5
Ebook ISBN 978-0-593-57902-2

The Library of Congress catalog record is available at https://lccn.loc.gov/2022032894.

Printed in China

waterbrookmultnomah.com

10 9 8 7 6 5 4 3 2 1

First Edition

Book and cover design by Sonia Persad

Most WaterBrook books are available at special quantity discounts for bulk purchase for premiums, fundraising,
and corporate and educational needs by organizations, churches, and businesses. Special books or book excerpts
also can be created to fit specific needs. For details, contact specialmarketscms@penguinrandomhouse.com.